CROOKS GALORE

Compiled by Pat Edwards and Wendy Body

Acknowledgements

We are grateful to the following for permission to reproduce copyright material: The Case of Natty Nat' from *Encyclopedia Brown, Boy Detective* by Donald J. Sobol (1963) is reprinted by permission of Angus & Robertson (UK); the author's agent for the story 'Things Go Wrong for The Red Tape Gang' from *The Adventures of The Red Tape Gang* by Joan Lowery-Nixon; Robson Books Ltd for the story 'Arthur and The Bellybutton Diamond' from *Arthur and the Bellybutton Diamond* by Alan Coren. Pages 38-9 were written by Bill Boyle.

We are grateful to the Metropolitan Police, London, for permission to reproduce the Neighbourhood Watch symbol on page 15 below right.

Illustrators include: Rebecca Parnell pp. 4-5; Brett Colquhoun pp. 6-13; David Wooodward pp. 14-15; Don Black pp. 16-35; Jenny Rendall pp. 36-7; Charles Front pp. 38-9; Michael Salter pp. 40-57; Melissa Webb pp. 58-9; Rachel Legge pp. 60-1; Loui Silvestro pp. 62-4.

CONTENTS

Bert the Burglar   *Pat Edwards*   4

Light-fingered Lou   *Pat Edwards*   5

The Case of Natty Nat   *Donald Sobol*   6

Five common crimes   14

Things Go Wrong for the Red Tape Gang
  Joan Lowery Nixon   16
    Part 1: The Secret Plan   16
    Part 2: A Dangerous Mistake   21
    Part 3: A New Member   32

Rules for secret clubs   36

Special days: Bonfire Night   38

Arthur and the Bellybutton Diamond
  Alan Coren   40

A page from Bertha Burglar's recipe book   58

Cop these!   59

What shall I be?   60

Ten famous criminals   62

Catch these words   *Glossary*   63

Bert the Burglar

Meet Bert the burglar
He's the bloke
who goes around stealing socks
He's tough as nails, the coppers say
and crafty as a fox.

He sneaks into your house
at night
through window or through door
and then makes off with any sock
left lying on the floor.

So when you hunt
and only find
just one sock of a pair,
that's when you know without a doubt
that Burglar Bert's been there.

Pat Edwards

4

Light-fingered Lou

Lost a sandwich?
Lost a shoe?
You must have met
Light-fingered Lou.

She'll pick a pocket,
pinch a purse,
or snatch your sweets
(and that is worse!)

So when you're standing
in a queue,
beware, beware
of you know who!

Pat Edwards

The Case of Natty Nat.

Mr and Mrs Brown had one child. They called him Leroy,
and so did his teachers. Everyone else in Idaville called him
Encyclopaedia.

An encyclopaedia is a book or a set of books giving
information, arranged alphabetically, on all branches of
knowledge.

Leroy Brown's head was like an encyclopaedia.
It was filled with facts he had learned from
books. He was like a complete library walking
around in sneakers.

Old ladies who did crossword puzzles were
always stopping him on the street to ask him
questions.

Just last Sunday, after church, Mrs Conway, the butcher's wife, had asked him: "What is a three-letter word for a Swiss river beginning with A?"

"Aar," Encyclopaedia answered after a moment.

He always waited a moment. He wanted to be helpful. But he was afraid that people might not like him if he answered their questions too quickly and sounded *too* clever.

His father asked him more questions that anyone else. Mr Brown was the chief of police of Idaville.

The town had four banks, three picture theatres, and a Little League. It had the usual number of petrol stations, churches, schools, shops, and comfortable houses on shady streets. It even had a mansion or two, and some dingy sections. And it had the average number of crimes for a community of its size.

Idaville, however, only *looked* like the usual American town. It was, really, most *un*usual.

For nearly a whole year no criminal had escaped arrest and no boy or girl had got away with breaking a single law in Idaville.

This was partly because the town's policemen were clever and brave. But mostly it was because Chief Brown was Encyclopaedia's father.

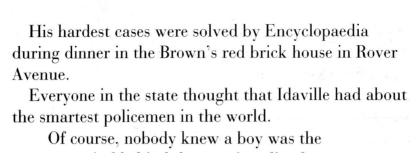

His hardest cases were solved by Encyclopaedia during dinner in the Brown's red brick house in Rover Avenue.

Everyone in the state thought that Idaville had about the smartest policemen in the world.

Of course, nobody knew a boy was the mastermind behind the town's police force.

You wouldn't guess it by looking at Encyclopaedia. He looked like almost any fifth-grade boy and acted like one, too — except that he never talked about himself.

Mr Brown never said a word about the advice his son gave him. Who would believe that his best detective was only ten years old?

This is how it began:

One evening at dinner, Mr Brown said,

"Natty Nat has struck again. He has held up another shop — and right here in Idaville."

"What shop, Dad?" asked Encyclopaedia.

"The Men's Shop, owned by Mr Dillon and Mr Jones," answered Mr Brown. "That makes six shops Natty Nat has held up in the state this month."

"Are you sure the robber was Natty Nat?" asked Encyclopaedia.

"Mr Dillon himself said it was Natty Nat," replied Mr Brown.

He pulled a notebook from his pocket and put it beside his plate. "I wrote down everything Mr Dillon told me about the holdup. I'll read it to you."

Encyclopaedia closed his eyes. He always closed his eyes when he was getting ready to think hard.

His father began to read what Mr Dillon, the shopkeeper, had told him about the holdup:

I was alone in the shop. I did not know anyone had come in. Suddenly a man's voice told me to raise my hands. I looked up then. I was face to face with the man the newspapers call Natty Nat. He had on a grey coat with a belt in the back, just as the newspapers said. He told me to turn and face the wall. Since he had a gun, I did as he said. When I turned around again, he was gone — with all the money.

Chief Brown finished reading and closed his notebook.

Encyclopaedia asked only one question: "Did the newspapers ever print a picture of Natty Nat?"

"No," answered his father. "He never stands still long enough for a picture to be taken. Remember, he's never been caught. But every policeman in the state knows he always wears that grey coat with the belt in the back."

"Nobody even knows his real name," said Encyclopaedia, half to himself. "Natty Nat is just what the newspapers call him."

Suddenly he opened his eyes. "Say, the only reason Mr Dillon thought it was Natty Nat was because of that grey coat!" he said. "The case is solved!"

"There is nothing to solve," objected Chief Brown. "There is no mystery. Mr Dillon was robbed. The holdup man was the same one who has been robbing other shops in the state."

"Not quite," said Encyclopaedia. "There was no holdup at The Men's Shop."

"What do you mean?" exclaimed Mr Brown.

"I mean Mr Dillon wasn't robbed, Dad. He lied from beginning to end," answered Encyclopaedia.

"Why should Mr Dillon lie?" demanded his father.

"I guess he spent the money. He didn't want his partner, Mr Jones, to know it was missing," said Encyclopaedia. "So Mr Dillon said he was robbed."

"Leroy," said his mother, "please explain what you are saying."

10

"It's simple, Mum," said Encyclopaedia. "Mr Dillon read all about Natty Nat in the newspapers. So he knew Natty Nat always wore a grey coat with a belt in the back when he held up shops."

"Go on, Leroy," said Mr Brown, leaning forward.

"Mr Dillon knew it would sound much better if he could blame his holdup on someone people have read about," said Encyclopaedia. "He said he knew it was Natty Nat because of the coat he wore —"

"That could be true," Chief Brown said.

"That *couldn't* be true," said Encyclopaedia. "Mr Dillon never saw the back of the man who held him up. He said so himself. Remember?"

Chief Brown frowned. He picked up his notebook again. He read to himself a while.

Then he shouted, "Leroy, I believe you are right!"

Encyclopaedia said, "Mr Dillon only saw the *front* of the holdup man. He had no way of knowing that the man's coat had a belt *in the back*!"

"He stole money from his own shop and from his partner too," cried Chief Brown. "And he nearly got away with it!"

He rushed from the dining room. "Leroy," said Mrs Brown, "did you get this idea from a television programme?"

"No," said Encyclopaedia. "I got it from a book I read about a great detective and his methods of observation."

"Well," said his mother proudly, "this proves how important it is to listen carefully and watch closely, to train your memory. Perhaps *you* will be a detective when you grow up."

"Mum," said Encyclopaedia, "can I have another piece of pie?"

Mrs Brown sighed. She had taught English in the Idaville High School before her marriage. "You *may* have another piece of pie," she said.

Donald J Sobol
illustrated by *Brett Colquhoun*

5 COMMON CRIME

 BURGLARY

(This means going into someone's house and stealing their property.)

THEFT

(Including shoplifting.)

CAR THEFT

SWAG

FRAUD OR FORGERY

(*Fraud* is when you deliberately trick someone so that you get their money or property. *Forgery* is when you sign a name that is not your own, or change a cheque so that the money is paid to you and not to the rightful person. It can also mean making false or counterfeit money.)

SERIOUS ASSAULT

(Injuring or hurting someone badly.)

HOW CAN YOU FIGHT CRIME?

Keep your eyes open! If you see anything suspicious, tell an adult immediately.

Never go with strangers. If you see a stranger trying to take away a younger child, tell an adult immediately.

Look after your property. If you have a bike, make sure that it is properly marked. Then, if it is stolen, you are more likely to get it back.

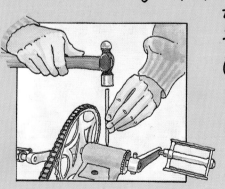

Find out if there is a Neighbourhood Watch scheme organised in the area where you live.

THINGS GO WRONG FOR THE Red Tape Gang

The Hartwells are not popular in Mike's house. Mr Hartwell has a huge hibiscus bush at the front of his house, which blocks the view of motorists. He refused the city council's request to trim the bush and Mike's father complains that because of "red tape" it will take months for the council to do anything.

To Mike, it seems a perfect chance for himself and his mates to do good. They call themselves "The Red Tape Gang" because their aim is to cut through "red tape" and get things done around the neighbourhood.

But there's another reason why the Hartwells are unpopular. Linda Jean Hartwell wants to join Mike's club . . .

PART 1:
The Secret Plan

We had just got inside our clubhouse and padlocked the front — well, the only — door, when the whole thing was ruined by old Linda Jean sticking her head in the side window and asking what we were doing.

"This is a club just for boys!" I yelled at her. "Go away!"

"Why does it have to be just for boys? I want to join too."

"Because that's the rules!" Leroy said.

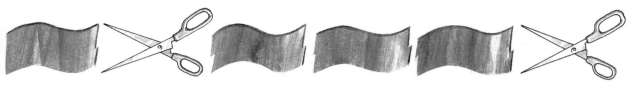

Linda Jean got mad. "You're discriminating against me!"

Leroy turned to look at me, a worried expression on his face. "Oh-oh! We don't want to discriminate. My pop says discrimination is the curse of the world."

"It is, if it's about black people, like you," I explained. "But it's perfectly legal to discriminate against girls."

His face brightened. "Are you sure?"

"I'm positive," I said. "There aren't any girls in the YMCA, are there?"

"That's right," Jimmy and Tommy said together.

Jimmy and Tommy are just ten months apart and in the same grade, and sometimes they act like a couple of twins.

"Okay then," Leroy said to Linda Jean. "We just voted you out!"

Linda Jean made a face at us. "All right for you! I'm going to shadow you! I'll be a spy and watch everything you do!"

We all tried to get out the door at once to catch her, but that was a big mistake, because Tommy and Leroy got stuck in the doorway, and three boards fell off, along with the padlock. By the time we got the doorway nailed back together again she had disappeared.

She wasn't kidding, though, when she said she was going to spy on us. Later she kept popping out from behind the garage every few minutes. We pretended we didn't see her, so she chucked a few dirt clods on the roof of the clubhouse.

18

While we were figuring what we'd have to do to get rid of her, we could hear her mother call her, three houses away.

"Linda Jean!" her mother yelled. "Come home and practise."

Her mother had a great pair of lungs. Mom said once that Mrs. Hartwell used to be a professional singer and pianist before she married Mr. Hartwell. She gave up on Linda Jean ever becoming a singer, but she had her practise the piano every day, hoping she'd someday be a pianist too. After I heard Linda Jean practising a couple of times, I could have told Mrs. Hartwell to save her money.

Linda Jean had to go home, and pretty soon we could hear that poor old piano thumping.

"As long as the piano is going, we're safe," Jimmy said.

"That girl is gonna grow up to be as mean as her old man," Tommy said.

That reminded me of the story in the newspaper, so I told Tommy and Jimmy about it.

"My dad said it would take months for the city to get anything done about that hibiscus bush," I said.

"I think somebody ought to help the city out," Leroy said. "Somebody could sneak out there at night and trim the bush, and nobody'd be the wiser."

"Yeah!" Tommy said. "And it would save the city a lot of trouble. Can't you just picture old Linda Jean's face when she looked out her window and the bush was cut back?"

We all laughed like crazy, until finally I guess the idea hit all of us at the same time.

"Every club ought to have some kind of purpose," I said.

"And our purpose could be to do good deeds," Tommy added.

"This could be a real good deed — even save lives if there weren't any more accidents at that corner," I said.

"Maybe we'd get a medal from the city," Jimmy suggested.

"Unh-unh," Leroy told him. "If we're going to do *that* kind of good, then we'd better keep quiet about it, or it'll spoil everything."

"That's what I think too," I said. "So let's meet tonight, after everybody is asleep, and take care of that bush!"

I began to feel a little shiver up my backbone after I had spoken the words, and I could tell that the others felt the same way.

"You think we can get away with it?" Jimmy whispered.

"Sure," I said. "If we meet at eleven, our parents will all be asleep, and I'll bring my dad's pruning shears."

Everyone was silent for a moment. Finally Leroy spoke up. "I'm coming."

"Me too," Tommy said.

Jimmy nodded. "Count me in." His eyes were wide. "What happens if we get caught?"

"We won't get caught," I said, trying to sound confident. I had wondered the same thing myself. There was no telling what might happen to us.

PART 2:

A Dangerous Mistake

I had a hard time staying awake, and I kept wondering what the other guys were doing. Mom came in and looked at me and patted the covers around my shoulders, even though I had pulled them up to my ears so she wouldn't notice I still had my clothes on.

Finally, their door shut, and in a little while everything was quiet.

I turned on my flashlight and looked at my watch. It was about ten thirty. So far everything was going all right. I quietly put my sneakers on and walked carefully out into the hall, moving one cautious step at a time. It was kind of hard to see in the dark.

At the bend in the hallway I bumped smack into my father. He let out a yell, and so did I. Quick as anything he grabbed my shoulder so hard that it hurt and flipped on the light switch. He had what was left of a glass of water in his hand. Most of it was dripping down his pyjamas.

My mother came running down the hall, crying, "Is it a burglar? Is it a burglar?"

She was waving a wooden coat hanger in one hand, and I guess I was glad enough I wasn't a burglar when I thought about how it would feel to be jumped on by my father, with my mother whacking away with a coat hanger.

They both looked surprised to see me. "Why, it's Michael!" Mom said. "What's going on? Why are you dressed?"

They were both staring at me, and I thought I had to say something, so I mumbled, "Isn't it morning yet?"

My mother chuckled and put her arms around me. "You poor thing," she laughed. "You just dreamed that it was morning."

"Is that what I did?"

"Yes, dear." She patted my shoulder. "Now you just take off your clothes and put on your pyjamas again and have a good night's sleep."

I went back into my bedroom and shut the door. I could hear the murmur of my parents' voices for a long time, and I kept turning on my flashlight and looking at my watch. It got closer and closer to eleven. If I didn't show up, the others would think I was scared, and they'd all go home.

Pretty soon it was two minutes to eleven. I opened my door carefully, so it wouldn't squeak, and listened.

Back in my parents' bedroom I could hear a little whistle with a rumble coming after it. My father was snoring, which meant if I were quiet enough, I could make it out the back door.

I felt my way along the dark hallway, inch by inch. I'd sure hate to run into anybody else!

Finally I made it to the kitchen and slowly opened the back door. I was afraid the screen door would make a noise, but my father has a thing about keeping stuff oiled and squeakless, so it opened without a sound. I gave a big sigh of relief.

Leroy was already in the clubhouse when I got there.

"Am I glad to see you!" he said. "It's spooky in here when it's dark."

"Do you think the others are coming?" I asked.

"What'll we do if they don't show?"

I shrugged. "We can do it ourselves."

But just then Tommy and Jimmy crawled in the doorway. Jimmy was rubbing his eyes.

"He fell asleep," Tommy said. "I had a terrible time waking him up without waking the whole house. He kept mumbling, 'Go away', so I finally put my hand over his mouth to keep him quiet, and he bit my finger."

"You can't blame people for things they do when they're asleep," Jimmy complained.

"Listen," I said, "it's already ten after eleven, and we haven't got much time." I had put the pruning shears in the clubhouse, and I felt around in the dark until I found them. "I've got the pruning shears right here."

Tommy felt them. "Are those ours? My dad's been griping at me, cause he can't find ours, and he thinks I had something to do with their being missing."

"No," I said, "they're ours. My dad puts his name on every tool he owns."

"I know why too," Leroy said. "Because when you left his hoe and rake over in the parkway and —"

"Never mind," I said. "If we're just going to sit around and tell dumb stories, we'll never get this job finished."

"Okay," Leroy said. "We're all set to go."

Single file, we crept through the yard and down the driveway and three houses away to the Hartwells' front yard. I hadn't taken a good look at the bush, and close to it, it looked sprawled out and big.

"No wonder this thing causes accidents," Jimmy said.

I decided how far down we should prune and got busy. The shears sounded awfully loud in the darkness, and we all looked around nervously.

We waited, but nothing happened, so I tried it again. The branches were thin and easy to cut, and it didn't take long until I was finished. I stepped back to admire the job.

"That's still too high," Leroy said. "You didn't take enough off."

The others nodded agreement, so Leroy took the pruning shears from me and set to work.

When he finished, the bush looked awful. It was ragged and shorter on one side than the other, so Tommy took the shears and tried it.

Jimmy kept objecting to the way Tommy was pruning the bush, so finally he had a turn. When he finished, that great big old hibiscus bush was only about two feet tall.

"We made a mistake," Tommy said.

"I'll say we did!" I answered.

"I mean, we shouldn't have just pruned it. First thing you know, the whole bush will grow back, and it will be as bad as it was before."

"You're right," Leroy said. "We should dig it up."

I examined what was left of the bush. I remembered how pretty it was when it was blooming. "If we just dug it up, that would be stealing," I said.

We all thought about that a minute. Then I had a great idea. "But how about if we dug it up and planted it some place else in their yard?"

"Good enough!" Leroy said.

I sent Jimmy back to my house to get the shovel, so we could dig, and in a few minutes he was back with it.

"Be careful of their sprinkler system," I warned. "It would be awful if we broke one of their pipes."

We all had to take turns digging, because that hibiscus had put down some big roots, but finally we got the thing loose.

"Now where do we put it?" Jimmy asked.

Tommy had been scouting around. "There's an empty space in an old flower bed next to their back porch. That would be a perfect place."

It was a good place, and the ground was soft enough so that it wasn't too hard to dig a hole.

We got the bush in and tamped down the dirt around it and were ready to congratulate ourselves for doing a good civic-minded job when Leroy blew the whole thing.

He dropped the shovel on the driveway, and it made a terrible clatter. A light flipped on in the Hartwell house.

We all froze. I was too scared to move.

We heard Mr. Hartwell yell, "Who's out there?" Before we could even think, he came rushing out on his porch, waving what looked like a gun.

"I see you!" he yelled.

I knew he really couldn't see us, because it was too dark, but the thought of a gun had me petrified.

"Stop!" he yelled, and he came charging toward us, right off that porch. When he fell into the hibiscus bush, he made a terrible noise.

Mrs. Hartwell was inside the house yelling, "Call the police!" And dumb old Linda Jean was calling, "Mama! Mama! Help!"

I grabbed the shovel, and Tommy, Jimmy, Leroy, and I ran away from that place so fast we could have broken the school track record.

"Scatter!" I yelled, and we did — each of us going to his own home.

I dropped the shovel on the grass in back and let myself into the kitchen door, my hands shaking so hard I didn't know how I'd get the door open. Somehow I managed to go quietly to my room without waking anyone, because I could still hear my father snoring.

I was too nervous to get undressed. I just took off my shoes and climbed under the blanket. I could hear a police siren coming down Santa Monica, and it stopped in front of the Hartwells'.

My father woke up and said, "Did you hear something?" But my mother just murmured at him, and they both went back to sleep.

I began to relax. The more I thought about it, the better I felt. We had cut through some red tape and accomplished what the city couldn't do without going to court. And Mr. Hartwell would get used to that bush being by his back steps and stop falling into it after a while. They'd never know who to thank.

I closed my eyes and got ready to go to sleep.

Then suddenly a thought hit me so hard I sat upright in bed, breaking into a cold sweat.

The police *would* know who was responsible, and they'd tell Mr. Hartwell, and maybe he'd come after me. *I had left the pruning shears, with my father's name on it, right there in plain sight!*

PART 3:
A New Member

Leroy, Tommy, Jimmy and me got together in a corner of
the schoolyard. I told them about the missing shears.

"Neither of us took it," Tommy said. "We just beat it out of
there. I've never been so scared in my life."

"I didn't take it," Leroy said.

"Okay," I said. "So what happened to it? If the police got it,
we'd be arrested by now. It didn't just fly away."

"Cool it," Leroy whispered. "Here comes Linda Jean."

We all stood there, trying not to see her, staring at the
school wall until she walked up and stopped.

"Hi," she said. "Are you talking about what happened at my
house last night?"

"Uh . . . we were talking about all sorts of things," I said.

"Do you know my father thinks there were four men and
they drove away in a white truck?"

"That was in the newspaper."

"It was exciting," she said. "My father got real mad at my
mother, because she called the police, and that was exciting
too."

"We heard the siren," Tommy said, but Jimmy nudged him, and he kept quiet.

"Were you talking about your club?" Linda Jean asked.

"Naw," I said.

"I want to join your club," she said.

"Look," I told her, "we already let you know that girls can't join our club!"

"Discrimination!" she sniffed.

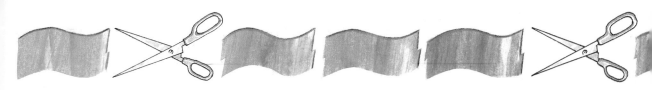

That word kept getting to Leroy. Right away his face got troubled, and he said, "Say, Mike, we don't want to get mixed up in any discrimination — even if it is just with girls."

"Leroy has the right idea," Linda Jean said.

"Leroy, I keep telling you that not letting girls in a club is not really discrimination," I said.

Linda Jean rubbed the toe of her shoe back and forth on the asphalt topping, making a little ridge in the sand that had blown over from the sandbox. "I could probably take it to the Supreme Court, but I won't," she said. "It doesn't make any difference if you do want to discriminate against me, because things are different now."

Tommy groaned. "You mean the Supreme Court has made rulings about boys' clubhouses?"

"I mean that now I've got the price of admission," she said.

We all started to laugh and holler. That was really funny! Price of admission! What did she think our clubhouse was — a movie theatre? That was the funniest thing we'd ever heard!

"My price of admission is a pair of pruning shears," she said.

We stopped laughing.

Jimmy looked at me. "What do we do, Mike?"

"Linda Jean Hartwell, you know that's blackmail!" I sputtered.

"No, it isn't," she said. "Not when people are discriminating against you."

Leroy frowned.

"You might even thank me for saving you," she added.

"How did you find the shears anyway?" Jimmy asked.

"Well," she said, "While my mother ran to help my father, I went down to the corner to look for the police. I ran right into the shears."

I sighed. "I don't think we have much choice. We'll have to let her into the club."

Everyone groaned except Linda Jean, who had the same kind of evil grin on her face as the mad scientist in the late movie I wasn't supposed to watch last week.

"Tell me why you cut down my father's hibiscus bush," she demanded, but the bell rang, and I muttered, "We'll tell you everything at the clubhouse after school today."

Joan Lowery Nixon
illustrated by *Don Black*

RULES FOR

KEEP OUT!

1. Don't have too many in the club.

2. Find a secret spot for meetings or build a club house at the bottom of someone's backyard.

3. Find a good name for your club (see next notice)

NAMES FOR CLUBS
- The clever kids club
- The secret six (or seven or eight)
- The geniuses
- The brainy bunch
- The marvellous mob
- The super snoopers
- The B.D.F.G. Team (use your initials)

5. Choose a secret password. Don't let anyone in to a meeting unless she or he can give the password. (suggestions: Bingo-bird, Flim-flam, Gusto, Frizzle, Varlet)
NB: It must be something no one else will guess. Look in a dictionary for other choices.

4. Decide what your club is going to do.
- Look for crime in the neighbourhood?
- Put on plays or shows like a backyard circus to raise money for charity?
- Produce a newspaper or magazine?

Daisy Chain Club

SECRET CLUBS

6. Decide on secret signs you can make to each other, e.g. a circle made with your thumb and forefinger means "I must talk to you in private."

7. Choose secret names for each other the way secret agents and spies do, e.g. Brown Mouse, Grey Feather, Samson, Four Square.

8. Make a special oath for everyone to take. It could be like this "I solemnly promise to be a loyal and true member of this club and never to tell any of its secrets to anyone. May my nose grow three times as long if I ever break this promise."

9. Make a list of rules for members to keep.

10. Find out how to write secret messages using milk, sugar, honey, orange or onion juice.

11. End the club as soon as it stops being fun.

James I

BONFIRE

Bonfire Night has been celebrated on 5th November since 1605, which was when James I was King of England. Here is the true story which explains why we remember this particular night in November.

REMEMBER, REMEMBER THE FIFTH OF NOVEMBER, GUNPOWDER, TREASON AND PLOT. I SEE NO REASON WHY GUNPOWDER TREASON SHOULD EVER BE FORGOT.

The Gunpowder Plot

1

James I angered Catholics because he had passed laws which made their lives and the practice of their religion more difficult. A group of Catholics, led by Robert Catesby, plotted to kill him.

2

Catesby's plan was to blow up the King and Parliament. Guy Fawkes who had used gunpowder while in the Spanish Army, joined the plotters.

The plotters hired a cellar underneath the House of Lords and placed barrels of gunpowder there, guarded by Guy Fawkes.

5

The King ordered his soldiers to search the Parliament buildings. They discovered Guy Fawkes and the gunpowder.

6

Guy Fawkes was thrown into a dungeon in the Tower of London and cruelly tortured to reveal the names of the other conspirators.

The conspirators were brought to trial, sentenced to death and executed.

Arthur
and the
Bellybutton Diamond

Thick, grey-green, oily-damp, the chill November
fog hung heavy over Baker Street. Through it,
though it was late morning, few sounds came: the
oddly muffled hoof of a cab-horse whose driver
was brave or foolish enough to be plying for hire;
the occasional tap-tap of a walking stick; far off,
the tinny squeak of a beggar's penny whistle; the
barking, here and there, of invisible London dogs;
and, from time to time, the yell of someone who
had walked into a lamp-post.

From his broad bay window upstairs at Number
221B, Sherlock Holmes stared out into the clammy
greyness, moodily; his unlit pipe hung from his
cheerless mouth, and the brightness in his keen
blue eyes was curiously bitter.

"A fine day for villains, Watson!" he burst out suddenly. "There is much dirty work being done out there today, invisible to the law!"

Doctor Watson, at the round table beside the crackling fire, merely dug a fork into his sixth kipper.

"The perfect day," he replied, "to stay in and eat, Holmes! I say, I've just realized I've polished off your breakfast, too, I really am most awfully—"

Holmes waved a bony hand impatiently.

"I have no appetite." he snapped. "There is only one thing I wish to get *my* teeth into, Watson, and that is a nice juicy case. Something with dreadful Oriental villains, perhaps; something with baffling codes to unravel; or a shocking international scandal, Watson, involving grisly headless corpses and—"

"I say, Holmes!" cried Watson. "Not when a chap's eating!"

Holmes glared at him.

"In that case," he muttered, "it is most unlikely that we shall ever be able to hold a serious conversation since there is no time when you are *not* eating!"

"That's most unfair, Holmes," replied Doctor Watson, slicing the top from his boiled egg, "I've got to get this breakfast eaten up, it'll be lunchtime before we know it; if I sit around chatting all the time what's going to happen to all these boiled eggs, never mind the toast and marmalade?"

Whether Sherlock Holmes intended to ignore this, or whether he would have preferred to throw his pipe at Doctor Watson, we shall never know. For at that very moment, there was a thunderous noise of hurrying boots upon the staircase outside, followed by an even more thunderous knocking at the door.

"Aha!" cried Sherlock Holmes, his face suddenly brightening. "Something would appear to be up! Come in, Inspector."

The door opened, and Inspector Lestrade of Scotland Yard burst breathlessly into the room. As always, his dark face bristled with suspicion.

"How," he bellowed, "did you know it was me?"

Sherlock Holmes smiled.

"Once I have heard a boot," he murmured, "I never forget it. A footstep, my dear Lestrade, is as individual as a finger-print. I have written three short books upon the subject, and I keep in my head the clear memory of some sixteen hundred and thirty-two feet."

"Amazing," mumbled Watson, through a large piece of smoked ham.

"Elementary," said Holmes. "If you remember, Watson, the case of the Giant Ferret of Whitechapel, you may recall that I identified the murderer from the noise of his left sock."

Watson burped, but in a very gentlemanly manner.

"I wonder," he murmured, delicately picking a toast crumb from his moustache, "whether Mrs Hudson has any kidneys up her sleeve?"

"Kidneys!" cried Inspector Lestrade, with such force that the plates piled around Doctor Watson jumped and rattled. "The Earl of Stepney's diamond tiepin 'as been stolen, nicked, knocked off, and generally, not to put too fine a point on it, pinched, and all you can talk about is bloomin' kidneys?"

The eagerness which had recently flushed Sherlock Holmes's thin cheeks suddenly paled.

"A tiepin?" he muttered. He walked stiffly to the window, hands clasped behind his back, and said, without turning his head, "I do not do tiepins. Nor, Inspector," and his voice was strangely tight, "do I do lost umbrellas, criminals suspected of travelling without a bus-ticket, or, for that matter, cats stuck up trees."

Doctor Watson waved a forkful of smoked haddock at Lestrade.

"You've upset him now, Inspector," he said. "You seem to forget that Mr Holmes is the greatest detective in the world."

"That's as maybe," snapped Lestrade, who preferred to think of Sherlock Holmes as the *second* greatest detective in the world, "but this is no ordinary tiepin, neither."

"*Either*," Holmes corrected, though in a polite murmur. He turned around. "And what, Inspector, makes this tiepin so extraordinary?"

"It 'appens to contain," replied Lestrade, "the Bellybutton Diamond!"

The effect of this upon Sherlock Holmes was remarkable!

"What!" he exclaimed. "But that is the largest diamond in the world! And surely it belongs to the Akond of Swat?"

"Who, or why, or which, or what," inquired Doctor Watson, "is the Akond of Swat?"

"He is a great South American ruler beloved of his people," answered Inspector Lestrade. "Or was."

"You mean he's dead?" asked Watson.

"No, I mean he's not beloved any more. They did not like 'im unscrewing the belly-button of their god, Dennis, and selling it to the Earl of Stepney. See, the Akond of Swat is barmy about clockwork trains. Can't get enough of 'em. I understand 'e has converted the top floor of his palace into a replica of Dalston Junction—eighty-eight miles of track, sixty-one engines, four hundred and twenty-two..."

"Oh, get on with it!" shouted Holmes, who, sensing the case was somewhat more curious than he had at first imagined, had grown very impatient. "Everyone knows what Dalston Junction looks like."

"Speak for yourself, Holmes," protested Watson. "Personally, I've never got further than its dining-room. Go on, Inspector."

"Well, clockwork trains cost money, I don't have to tell you that, and the Akond was running a bit short last year. So he looked around for something to sell, and he reckoned this big marble statue of Dennis outside Swat town hall didn't need a diamond belly-button, so 'e unscrewed it and flogged it to the Earl of Stepney. Who 'ad it made into a tiepin."

"Curiouser and curiouser!" muttered Sherlock Holmes (whose favourite book was *Alice in Wonderland*). He began to pace up and down. "It is my understanding that the Bellybutton Diamond is the size of a man's fist. How on earth can the Earl of Stepney wear it on his tie?"

"With great difficulty," replied Lestrade. "'E is only a little bloke, and 'is head keeps getting dragged forward with the weight. But 'e's got his reasons for wearing it, Mr Holmes, and very peculiar reasons they are, too, I don't mind saying."

"You will have to explain them in the cab," cried Holmes, snatching his cape and deerstalker hat from their pegs. "There is no time to be lost, Inspector! We must hurry to the scene of what I fear may turn out to be a very terrible crime indeed!"

But as he and Lestrade waited somewhat irritably while Doctor Watson eased his podgy bulk away from the breakfast table and struggled into his enormous coat and wrapped some cold sausages in his napkin for the journey, more footsteps sounded outside, followed by a polite knock.

"Who's this, Holmes?" said Watson.

Holmes frowned.

"I've no idea," he replied. "The shoes are entirely unfamiliar."

He pulled the door open.

A small boy stood there. He raised his hat politely.

"Good morning, Mr Holmes," said Arthur.

"Good morning, Arthur," said the great detective. "You have new shoes, I hear."

Arthur nodded.

"And you, Mr Holmes," he said, "are about to call on the Earl of Stepney."

"Good heavens!" cried Watson. "However did you know that?"

"'E prob'ly listens at key 'oles," muttered Lestrade, who did not like small boys.

"Come, come, my dear Inspector," said Sherlock Holmes sternly, "you know Arthur better than that."

"Humph!" humphed the policeman. For he *did*
know Arthur better than that; which was half the
trouble, because he had met Arthur, as those of
you who have read *Arthur and the Great Detective*
may remember, on board the S. S. *Murgatroyd*,
when Arthur had managed to solve a remarkably
tricky crime that had baffled not only Inspector
Lestrade, which was to be expected, but also
Sherlock Holmes, which was not. And while
Holmes was a generous person who was delighted
that a small boy had succeeded where he had
failed, Inspector Lestrade was a rather small-
minded person, who hated being outdone,
particularly by children.

So he said to Arthur now:

"Well then, clever dick, if you *wasn't* listening at
key 'oles, 'ow, may I ask, did you know about the
Earl of Stepney?"

"Because," said Arthur, "at nine o'clock this morning, I learned that the Bellybutton Diamond had been stolen, so I –"

"But," cried the agitated Lestrade, "the police themselves didn't find out till nine-fifteen! A small boy run all the way with the message!"

"*Ran* all the way," corrected Arthur, even more quietly and politely than Sherlock Holmes had done. 'Yes, he did. He was one of my Baker Street Irregulars."

"And what," snorted Lestrade scornfully, "might *they* be when they're at home?"

"When they're at home," replied Arthur, "they're just small boys. But when they're out and about the streets of London for me and Mr Holmes, they're detectives and spies and messengers and almost anything you care to think of. We're a network, aren't we, Mr Holmes?"

"That you are, Arthur," nodded the great detective, "and a most valuable one. There is much that an unobtrusive small boy may see and hear, Lestrade, that a large and, er, noisy policeman may not. Such as the first news of the Bellybutton Diamond affair, eh, Arthur? But come, we are wasting valuable time! Arthur, since you were in at the start of things you had better accompany us to Stepney Castle."

"Right!" said Arthur. "I'll just fetch my magnifying glass."

Inspector Lestrade rolled his eyes.

"And how long will *that* take?" he groaned.

"Only a moment," replied Arthur. "I live upstairs."

"Upstairs?" echoed Lestrade. "You mean at –"

"221A," said Arthur.

Outside, the dank fog folded them in. Even to one another, standing close, they became little more than silhouettes, four oddly assorted shapes in the silent swirling gloom. It must be like this under the sea, thought Arthur. Above them, a gaslight hung, strangely disembodied from its post by the fog and still glowing yellow, the lamplighter having not yet come by, because of the weather, to turn it out. Its light was worse than none at all; it shed an eeriness, distorting shadows, conjuring odd visions in the shifting veils of fog.

"There will be murders today," murmured
Sherlock Holmes.

"Blow murders!" cried Doctor Watson, stout
and cheery as ever. "Will there be cabs, is what I

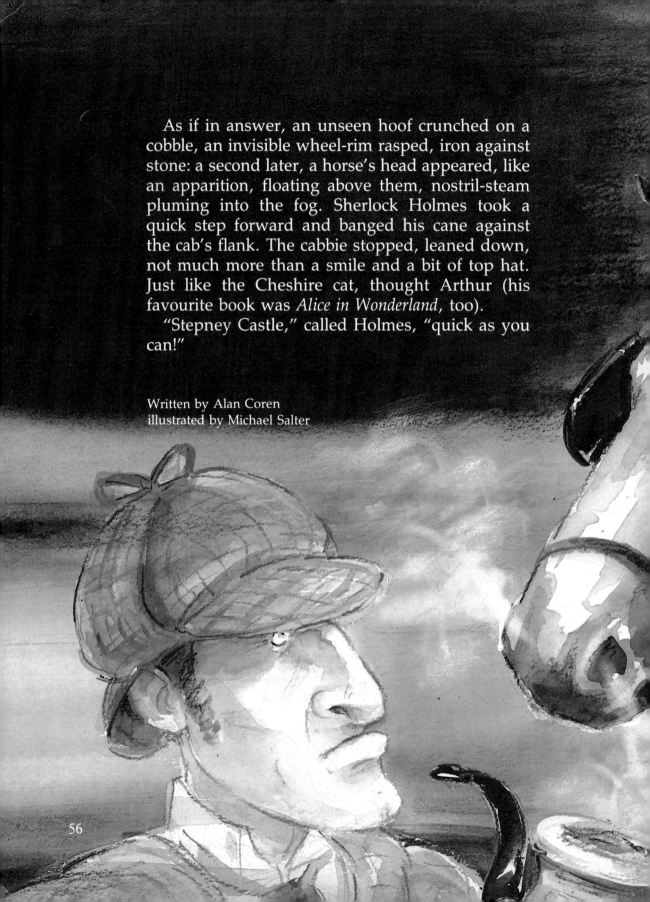

As if in answer, an unseen hoof crunched on a cobble, an invisible wheel-rim rasped, iron against stone: a second later, a horse's head appeared, like an apparition, floating above them, nostril-steam pluming into the fog. Sherlock Holmes took a quick step forward and banged his cane against the cab's flank. The cabbie stopped, leaned down, not much more than a smile and a bit of top hat. Just like the Cheshire cat, thought Arthur (his favourite book was *Alice in Wonderland*, too).

"Stepney Castle," called Holmes, "quick as you can!"

Written by Alan Coren
illustrated by Michael Salter

56

You can read more about Arthur in
Arthur and the Bellybutton Diamond by Alan Coren
published by Puffin

A PAGE FROM

BERTHA BURGLAR'S RECIPE BOOK

Bert's Special Fruit Cake

Find a cake tin at least 30cm long. Line with greaseproof paper and sprinkle the bottom with a little baking powder to stop fruit sinking.

227g Butter or margarine
227g Brown sugar
2 tablespoons Golden Syrup
1 tablespoon Marmalade
5 Eggs
340g Flour
Pinch of salt
1 teaspoon Baking powder
680g Mixed fruit
56g Mixed peel
1 teaspoon Spice
½ teaspoon Nutmeg
Pinch of ground cloves

1 large file for filing through prison bars.

Cream butter or margarine and sugar, add golden Syrup and marmalade. Gradually add well-beaten eggs with the sifted dry ingredients. Add prepared fruit. Bake 2½ hours at 165°C or 325°F. N.B. Remember to warn Bert that next time he's not to cut the cake in front of the warders.

59

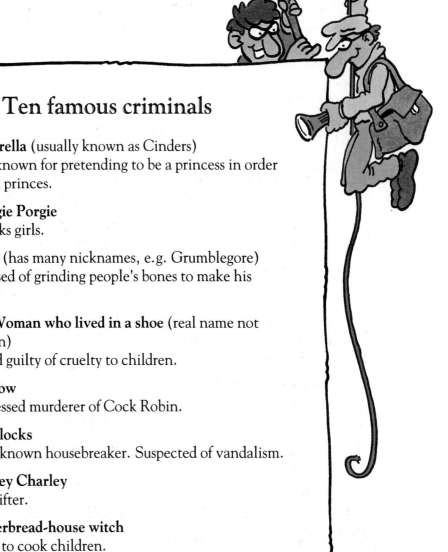

Ten famous criminals

1 Cinderella (usually known as Cinders)
Well known for pretending to be a princess in order to fool princes.

2 Georgie Porgie
Attacks girls.

3 Giant (has many nicknames, e.g. Grumblegore)
Accused of grinding people's bones to make his bread.

4 Old Woman who lived in a shoe (real name not known)
Found guilty of cruelty to children.

5 Sparrow
Confessed murderer of Cock Robin.

6 Goldilocks
Well-known housebreaker. Suspected of vandalism.

7 Charley Charley
Shoplifter.

8 Gingerbread-house witch
Tried to cook children.

9 Goosey Gander
Trespasser. Also assaulted old man.

10 Mother Hubbard
Accused by RSPCA* of cruelty to dog.

* RSPCA — Royal Society for the Prevention of Cruelty to Animals

Catch these Words

Glossary

accomplished *(p. 30)*
done

apparition *(p. 56)*
ghost

branches of knowledge *(p. 6)*
subjects

civic-minded *(p. 28)*
doing the best thing
for your town or city

conspirator *(p. 38)*
someone who plots with
other people

crafty *(p. 4)*
cunning

dingy *(p. 7)*
run-down and dirty

discriminating against
(p. 17)
treating someone
differently (usually less
well)

entomologist *(p. 60)*
someone who studies insects

griping *(p. 25)*
grumbling

Little League *(p. 7)*
children's baseball team

murmur *(p. 30)*
low sound

network *(p. 53)*
a group whose members
are connected in
some way

observation *(p. 13)*
watching and
listening carefully

petrified *(p. 28)*
terrified

Glossary continues on page 64

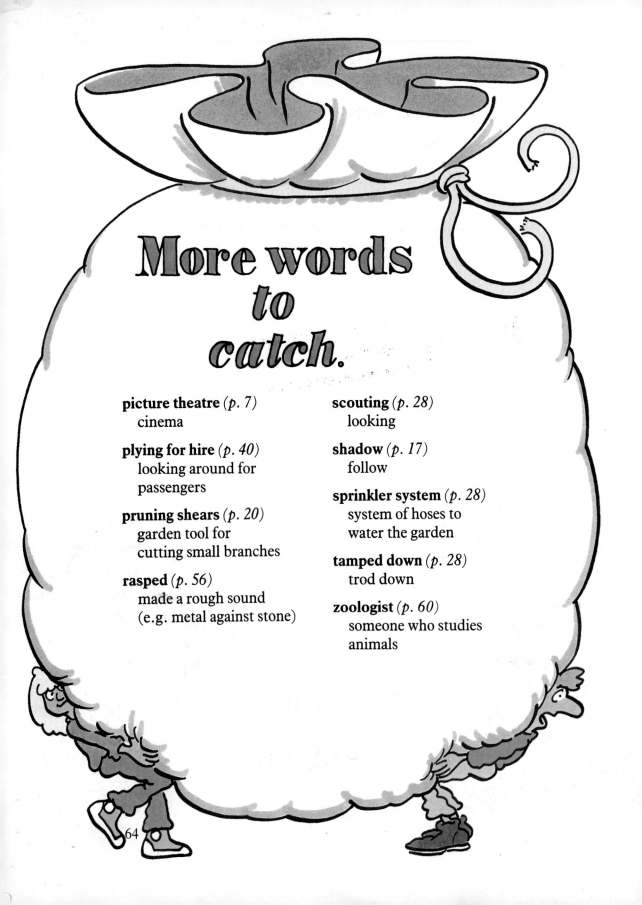

More words to catch.

picture theatre (*p. 7*)
cinema

plying for hire (*p. 40*)
looking around for
passengers

pruning shears (*p. 20*)
garden tool for
cutting small branches

rasped (*p. 56*)
made a rough sound
(e.g. metal against stone)

scouting (*p. 28*)
looking

shadow (*p. 17*)
follow

sprinkler system (*p. 28*)
system of hoses to
water the garden

tamped down (*p. 28*)
trod down

zoologist (*p. 60*)
someone who studies
animals